T0080610

PROTEIN on MyPlate

by Mari Schuh
Consulting editor: Gail Saunders-Smith, PhD

Consultant: Barbara J. Rolls, PhD
Guthrie Chair in Nutrition
Pennsylvania State University
University Park, Pennsylvania

CAPSTONE PRESS
a capstone imprint

Pebble Plus is published by Capstone Press,
1710 Roe Crest Drive, North Mankato, Minnesota 56003.
www.capstonepub.com

Copyright © 2013 by Capstone Press, a Capstone imprint. All rights reserved.
No part of this publication may be reproduced in whole or in part, or stored in a retrieval system, or transmitted in any form or by any means, electronic, mechanical, photocopying, recording, or otherwise, without written permission of the publisher. For information regarding permission, write to Capstone Press,
1710 Roe Crest Drive, North Mankato, MN 56003.

The author dedicates this book to Devon Borst of Pleasant Prairie, Wisconsin,
who makes the best hard-boiled eggs in southeastern Wisconsin.

Library of Congress Cataloging-in-Publication Data
Schuh, Mari C., 1975–
Protein on myplate / by Mari Schuh.
p. cm.—(Pebble plus. What's on myplate?)
Includes bibliographical references and index.
Summary: "Simple text and photos describe USDA's MyPlate tool and healthy protein choices for children"—Provided by publisher.
ISBN 978-1-4296-8745-4 (library binding)
ISBN 978-1-4296-9420-9 (paperback)
1. Proteins in human nutrition—Juvenile literature. I. Title.
TX553.P7S38 2013
612'.01575—dc23 2012009315

Editorial Credits
Jeni Wittrock, editor; Sarah Bennett, designer; Svetlana Zhurkin, media researcher; Kathy McColley, production specialist; Sarah Schuette, photo stylist; Marcy Morin, studio scheduler

Photo Credits
All photos by Capstone Studio/Karon Dubke except:
Shutterstock: BW Folsom, cover (bottom left), Igor Klimov, cover (top right), Pshenichka, cover (bottom right), Tristan Tan, back cover; USDA, cover (inset), 5

Information in this book supports the U.S. Department of Agriculture's MyPlate food guidance system found at www.choosemyplate.gov. Food amounts listed in this book are based on daily recommendations for children ages 4-8. The amounts listed in this book are appropriate for children who get less than 30 minutes a day of moderate physical activity, beyond normal daily activities. Children who are more physically active may be able to eat more while staying within calorie needs. The U.S. Department of Agriculture (USDA) does not endorse any products, services, or organizations.

Note to Parents and Teachers

The What's on MyPlate? series supports national science standards related to health and nutrition. This book describes and illustrates the USDA's recommendations on protein. The images support early readers in understanding the text. The repetition of words and phrases helps early readers learn new words. This book also introduces early readers to subject-specific vocabulary words, which are defined in the Glossary section. Early readers may need assistance to read some words and to use the Table of Contents, Glossary, Read More, Internet Sites, and Index sections of the book.

Printed in the United States 5469

Table of Contents

MyPlate 4
Protein 6
Enjoying Protein Foods 14
How Much to Eat 22

Glossary 23
Read More 23
Internet Sites 24
Index 24

MyPlate

Protein foods are
an important part of MyPlate.
MyPlate is a tool that helps
you choose healthful food.

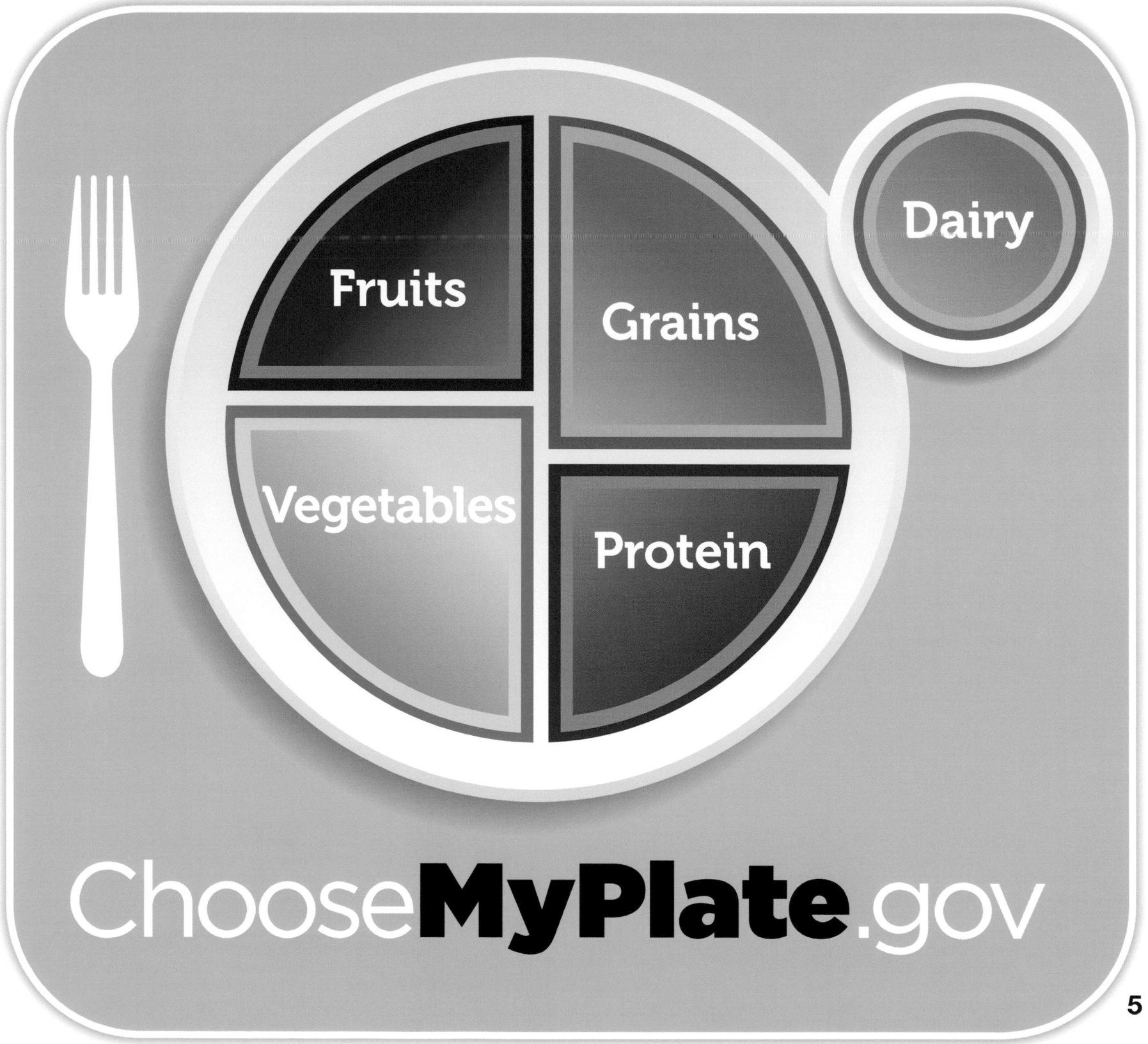
Fruits
Grains
Dairy
Vegetables
Protein
ChooseMyPlate.gov

Protein

Meats like chicken, beef,
and fish are protein foods.
Beans, eggs, nuts, and seeds
are also full of protein.

Protein helps build
bones and muscles.
Protein-rich foods
are full of nutrients.

Every day, eat 4 ounces (110 grams) of protein. Try to eat different protein foods every week.

Eat lean protein.

Lean protein is low in fat.

Have an adult trim away

the fat from meat

before cooking.

Enjoying Protein Foods

Good morning!

Start the day with protein.

Eat ham and eggs

for breakfast.

PUSH UP
HERE
Nutrition Facts

Mixed nuts make
a crunchy snack.
Sprinkle nuts
on frozen yogurt.

It's lunchtime.

Make a sandwich.

Choose peanut butter,

tuna, sliced lean meat,

or a veggie burger.

On a cold night,
warm up with chili
made with meat and beans.
What protein foods
will you choose tomorrow?

How Much to Eat

Many kids need to eat about 4 ounces (110 grams) of protein every day. To get 4 ounces, pick four servings of your favorite foods below.

¼ cup (60 mL) refried beans

½ ounce (15 grams) sunflower seeds

2 tablespoons (30 mL) hummus

½ veggie burger

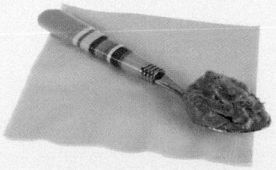

1 tablespoon (15 mL) peanut butter

1 egg

1 ounce (30 grams) tuna

1 slice lean turkey

Glossary

muscle—a tissue in the body that is made of strong fibers; muscles can be tightened or relaxed to make the body move

MyPlate—a food plan that reminds people to eat healthful food and be active; MyPlate was created by the U.S. Department of Agriculture

nutrient—something that people need to eat to stay healthy and strong; vitamins and minerals are nutrients

protein—a substance found in plant and animal cells; your body needs protein to stay healthy

veggie burger—a burger made from vegetables, soybeans, and nuts; veggie burgers do not have any meat in them

Read More

Adams, Julia. *Proteins.* Good Food. New York: PowerKids Press, 2011.

Borgert-Spaniol, Megan. *Protein Foods Group.* Eating Right with MyPlate. Minneapolis: Bellwether Media, 2012.

Lee, Sally. *The Powerful Protein Group.* MyPlate and Healthy Eating. Mankato, Minn.: Capstone Press, 2012.

Internet Sites

FactHound offers a safe, fun way to find Internet sites related to this book. All of the sites on FactHound have been researched by our staff.

Here's all you do:

Visit *www.facthound.com*

Type in this code: 9781429687454

Index

bones, 8
breakfast, 14
fat, 12
lean proteins, 12
lunch, 18
muscles, 8
MyPlate, 4
nutrients, 8
servings, 10, 22
snacks, 16

Word Count: 146
Grade: 1
Early-Intervention Level: 15